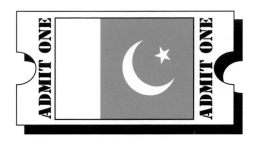

FACES
AND
PLACES

PAKISTAN

BY SHARON SHARTH

THE CHILD'S WORLD®

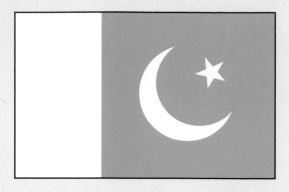

GRAPHIC DESIGN

Robert E. Bonaker / Graphic Design & Consulting Co.

PAGE PRODUCTION

The Design Lab

PHOTO RESEARCH

Dawn Friedman

PHOTO CREDITS

Cover: Keren Su/Corbis; Sayyid Azim/AP Wide World Photos: 27; Gerard Degeorge/Corbis: 2; John R. Jones; Papilio/Corbis: 8, 22; Galen Rowell/Corbis: 9, 16; Ric Ergenbright/Corbis: 11, 23; Bettmann/Corbis: 13; Reuters NewMedia, Inc./Corbis: 15, 17; Bennett Dean; Eye Ubiquitous/Corbis: 19; AFP/Corbis: 20, 26; Jonathan Blair/Corbis: 21; Staffan Widstrand/Corbis: 24; Nik Wheeler/Corbis: 25; Zahid Hussein, Reuters/Getty Images: 10; Hulton Archive/Getty Images: 12; Getty Images: 14; Anis Hamdi, Newsmakers/Getty Images: 18; Alex Wong/Getty Images: 29.

PROJECT COORDINATION

Editorial Directions, Inc.

Library of Congress Cataloging-in-Publication Data
Sharth, Sharon.
Pakistan / by Sharon Sharth.
p. cm.
Summary: An introduction to the geography, history, plant and animal life, and social
life and customs of Pakistan.
Includes bibliographical references and index.
Contents: Where is Pakistan?—The land—Plants and animals—Long ago—Pakistan
today—The people—City life and country life—Schools and language—Work—Food—Pastimes and holidays.
ISBN 1-56766-637-X (library bound : alk. paper)
1. Pakistan—Juvenile literature. [1. Pakistan.] I. Title.
DS376.9.S47 2003
954.91—dc21
2002151511

Table of Contents

Where Is Pakistan?

Western Hemisphere

PAKISTAN

Pakistan (White) Is In The East And U.S.A. (Cream) Is In The West

Eastern Hemisphere

Earth is made up of landmasses surrounded by water. The seven largest landmasses are called continents. Asia is the largest continent. Pakistan (PAH-kis-taan) is a country in the southern part of Asia. India lies to the east. Afghanistan and Iran are to the west. The Arabian Sea touches Pakistan's border to the south. China lies to the north. Pakistan is about twice as big as the state of California in the United States.

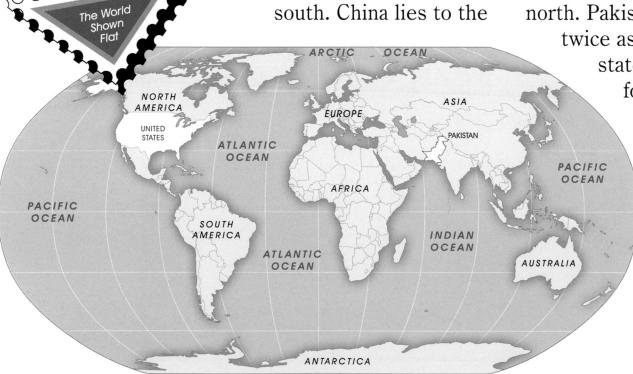

The World Shown Flat

ARCTIC OCEAN

NORTH AMERICA

UNITED STATES

ATLANTIC OCEAN

EUROPE

ASIA

PAKISTAN

PACIFIC OCEAN

AFRICA

PACIFIC OCEAN

SOUTH AMERICA

ATLANTIC OCEAN

INDIAN OCEAN

AUSTRALIA

ANTARCTICA

TURKMENISTAN

UZBEKISTAN

TAJIKISTAN

CHINA

Close-Up
Of
Pakistan

AFGHANISTAN

Indus River

★ Islamabad

Lahore •

Sutlej River

IRAN

Indus River

P A K I S T A N

INDIA

NEPA

Dasht R.

Hyderabad •

N

W   E

S

Karachi •

| 0 | | 100 | | 200 miles |
| 0 | 100 | | 200 kilometers | |

Arabian Sea

The Valley
Of The Indus
River In
Northern
Pakistan

Islamabad
Lahore
Indus R.
Sutlej R.
Indus River
Dasht R.
Hyderabad
Karachi

Most of Pakistan is hot, dry desert. If you travel to the northern part of the country, however, the land and weather are not at all like a desert. You will find rocky land and freezing temperatures.

Three mountain ranges cross northern Pakistan. One of them is the Karakoram mountain range. This is where you will find K2, the second-highest mountain in the world.

The mighty Indus River runs through the country. Most of the people of Pakistan—called Pakistanis (pahk-ih-STAHN-eez)—live along its shores in the Indus Valley. Flooding sometimes occurs here during the heavy rains of July and August. This is the rainy season.

The Frozen Slopes Of The Karakoram Mountain Range

In some of the northern parts of Pakistan, snow leopards, musk deer, wild sheep, and hyenas live in the pine forests. Fish, ducks, geese, and many other kinds of birds live in and around the lakes at the foothills of the mountains.

In the dry deserts farther south, few plants are able to grow. The camel is one of the few animals that can live in the hot, dry climate. In the cooler areas, many farmers raise animals, such as goats and sheep. A wealthy

Pakistani family in the countryside may own two water buffalo, two oxen, goats, sheep, and a few chickens.

Traveling Camels In The Deserts Of Eastern Pakistan

A Pakistani Farmer Plows His Fields With Oxen.

Islamabad

Lahore

Indus R.

Sutlej R.

Indus River

Dasht R.

Hyderabad

Karachi

The Signing Of The Document That Created The Country Of Pakistan In 1947

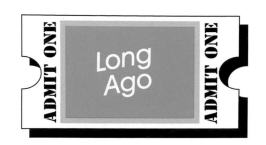

Long Ago

Hindus Leave Pakistan For India In 1947.

People have lived in what is now Pakistan for thousands of years. Scientists have found **remains** that are more than 5,000 years old!

The land of Pakistan was once part of India. From the early 1500s until 1858, **Muslim** emperors called Mughals (MOO-gulz) ruled India. Some Indians followed their religion, called Islam (IS-lahm), but most Indians were **Hindus.**

In 1858, Britain took control of India. When the Indian people won their independence from Britain in 1947, the Muslims demanded their own country. It was agreed that the Muslims would use part of India's land to create an Islamic state.

About one million Muslims and Hindus were killed as the countries of India and Pakistan were established. At that time, Pakistan was made up of East Pakistan and West Pakistan. About 1,000 miles (1,609 kilometers) of Indian land separated these two areas. In 1971, a civil war was fought when East Pakistan declared it was an independent country called Bangladesh.

Pakistan Today

The Pakistanis and the Indians are still fighting. Today, the disagreement is over the state of Kashmir (kash-MEER) in northern Pakistan. Because most people in Kashmir are Muslims, Pakistanis believe the land belongs to them. Indians believe Kashmir is Indian land, however. Pakistan and India have been at war with each other four times since 1947.

The president of Pakistan is General Pervez Musharraf. He took over the country in a military **coup** in 1999. Whoever has the support of the army usually rules the country. India's leader was chosen in national elections. Pakistan and India both have nuclear weapons that could be used in a war. It is important for the leaders of these two countries to seek peace.

Pakistani President General Pervez Musharraf

People View Their Destroyed House In Pakistani-Held Kashmir In 2002.

A Pakistani Family In Its Home In The Karakoram Mountains Of Pakistan

Karakoram Mtns
Indus R.
Islamabad
Lahore
Sutlej R.
Indus River
Dasht R.
Hyderabad
Karachi

The People

About 145 million people live in Pakistan. That number continues to grow. That is more than half as many people as there are in the United States.

Most Pakistanis are very poor. However, they have close family ties. Many relatives, including married sons and their families, may live together in one house. Nearly all marriages are arranged by the couple's parents.

From 1988 to 1990 and from 1993 to 1996, the prime minister of Pakistan was a woman named Benazir Bhutto. But few Pakistani women work outside their homes. Some women wear a simple shawl across their shoulders. Others wear a **burqa** that covers their bodies completely. Many laws in Pakistan still keep women from being treated fairly.

Pakistani Women Wearing Burqas That Completely Cover Their Bodies

City Life and Country Life

Crowded streets lined with open-air shops are found in Pakistani cities. Spices, jewelry, flowers, radios, and vegetables are all for sale in these shops. In the city, families of nine or ten may live in two small rooms. Poor Pakistanis may share a bathroom and a **courtyard** with other families. Houses often have no electricity and no running water. Many times during the day, women fill jugs with clean water from a faucet down the street. Many areas have no sewers, so diseases are common. Men often work in factories or shops while women stay at home.

Most Pakistanis live in country villages. Farmers plow the land with oxen. Their wives take care of the home, the children, and the livestock. Other men in the village may be tailors, carpenters, potters, weavers, or shoemakers. Families live in simple huts with mud walls. Inside, the rooms are dark and bare. The huts are built close together so families can share a well. A pump pulls the water from the well. Power for the well comes from connecting a blindfolded camel or ox to the pump. The camel or ox then walks in a circle to make the pump work.

Women And Children Search For Water In Karachi

A Cobbler In Bahawalpur

Islamabad ★

Lahore

Sutlej R.

Indus River

Indus R.

Dasht R.

Hyderabad

Karachi

An Urdu Language Newspaper In 2001

Schools and Language

Pakistani children start school when they are five years old. Most never finish the fifth grade. This means that more than half of the Pakistani people cannot read or write.

There are many reasons for this problem. There are not enough schools or teachers in Pakistan.

In many areas, one-room schoolhouses are crowded with students who do not have desks or schoolbooks. Sometimes children are taught outside because their village has no schoolhouse.

Many people in Pakistan speak Punjabi (pun-JAH-be). The official language of Pakistan is Urdu (UR-doo). Most Pakistanis are bilingual and many other **dialects** and languages are spoken throughout the country. A small number of well-educated Pakistanis, including people in the government and military leaders, speak English.

Pakistani Boys and Girls Reading In An Outdoor Class

Most Pakistanis live in the desert near the Indus River. Many are farmers. They have **irrigated** the land to water their crops. This area has one of the largest irrigation systems in the world.

Wheat is Pakistan's main crop. Sugarcane, rice, and cotton are also grown in the Indus River valley. The production of cotton cloth and the manufacturing of clothes are Pakistan's largest industries.

A few women in Pakistan have become lawyers and doctors. Some own their own businesses, but most women stay at home. Women may spend all day cooking for their large families. They must wash clothes and get water. Girls help care for the younger children and milk the water buffalo. Boys work with their fathers in the fields or shops.

A Pakistani Woman Cooks Bread In Her Home.

Islamabad ★
Lahore •
Indus R.
Indus River
Sutlej R.
Dasht R.
Karachi • Hyderabad •

Pakistani Rice
Fields

A Man
Sells Food In The
Street In Karachi.

Peshawar

Islamabad ★

Indus R.

Lahore

Sutlej R.

Indus River

Dasht R.

Hyderabad

Karachi

44 Mills
NAV DURGA TEXTILES 456 COLOURS

Food

The food of Pakistan is rich and spicy. Pakistani women buy a variety of spices and blend them together with water to make a paste. They cook the spices in *ghee* (GEE), which is melted butter made from water-buffalo milk. Then they add meat or vegetables. Few Pakistanis can afford meat more than once a week, so vegetables are their main food. Lentils, spinach, onions, green beans, cauliflower, peas, and carrots are some favorite foods. They usually are mixed with spices. Most Pakistanis do not use forks or spoons. Instead, they scoop up food with pieces of bread.

Mangos, oranges, melons, and other fresh fruits are often served for dessert. A popular sweet made from boiled milk is called *ras gulahs* (rahs GUL-lahz). Balls of the sugared milk are cooked in hot syrup and cooled before eating. Rice pudding is also a favorite dessert.

Spices, Dried Roots, And Fruit For Sale In Peshawar

Pastimes and Holidays

ADMIT ONE · ADMIT ONE

Long ago, Muslim musicians created what today is called South Asian music. They invented the *sitar*, a long, stringed instrument, and the *tabla*, two small drums. The most popular music in Pakistan is from Indian movies. Favorite sports include cricket, hockey, tennis, polo, and squash.

Eid al-Azha is an important Muslim holiday. For this holiday, wealthy families kill more than 3 million goats in the name of Allah. One-third of the meat goes to the poor. During Ramadan, Muslims **fast** from sunrise to sunset. They celebrate the holiday of *Eid al-Fitr* at the end of Ramadan with gift giving, sweets, and family gatherings.

There is much fighting in Pakistan today between Muslims and non-Muslims. Travel is difficult, even dangerous.

The leaders of Pakistan and India need to find a way to solve their problems so the people can live in peace. Then more travelers will be able to experience Pakistan's fascinating culture.

Muslims Praying

Peshawar
Islamabad ★
● Rawalpindi
Faisalabad ●
Lahore ●

Indus R.

Indus River / Sutlej R.

Dasht R.

Hyderabad ●

Karachi ●

Pakistani
Cricketeer
Misbah
ul Haq

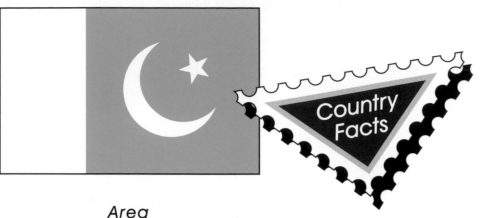

Area
307,374 square miles (796,099 square kilometers).

Population
About 145 million people.

Official Name
Islamic Republic of Pakistan.

Capital City
Islamabad.

Other Important Cities
Faisalabad, Karachi, Hyderabad, Lahore, Peshawar, Rawalpindi.

Money
Rupee (roo-PEE).

Official Language
Urdu.

Religion
97 percent Muslim and 3 percent Hindus, Christians, and others.

National Flag
The flag is bright green with a stripe of white on the left side. Over the green background, a white star hovers inside the arms of a white crescent moon.

National Anthem
"Pak Sarzameen Shad Bad" ("Blessed Be the Sacred Land").

Head of State
The president of Pakistan.

A
Painted
Pakistani
Bus

Did You Know?

In 1970, a cyclone hit East Pakistan. This cyclone produced an enormous, destructive wave called a tsunami. More than 260,000 people were killed.

K2 is 28,250 feet (8,611 meters) high. The peak is covered by snow and usually cannot be seen because it is in the clouds.

Benazir Bhutto, the former prime minister of Pakistan, was the first woman to lead the government of an Islamic country. She was born in the city of Karachi and studied in the United States at Harvard University.

Muhammad, the **prophet** and founder of Islam, was born in the city of Mecca (in Saudi Arabia) around 570. Muslims believe that Allah—their God—chose Muhammad as his messenger. Allah revealed the teachings of the Qu'ran—the holy book of Islam—to him. Muhammad died in 632.

Islam teaches that Muslims must spread their religion throughout the world. Some Muslims believe that Allah wants them to fight against people who are not Muslims. Some Muslim children are even taught that they please Allah if they die fighting for Islam.

How Do You Say?

ENGLISH	URDU	HOW TO SAY IT IN URDU
Hello	adaab arz	ADAAB URZ
Goodbye	allah hafiz	ALLAH HA-fiz
Thank You	shukriya	shook-ree-yaa
One	ek	AYK
Two	do	DO (rhymes with so)
Three	tin	TEEN
Land of the Pure	Pakistan	PAH-kis-taan
Cat	billi	BILL-lee

burqa (BER-kah)
Muslim women sometimes wear a dress that covers their bodies from head to toe. This dress is called a burqa.

coup (KOO)
When the military suddenly overthrows the government, it is called a military coup. President Pervez Musharraf of Pakistan took over the country in this way.

courtyard (KORT-yard)
An open space that is in the middle of or partly surrounded by buildings is called a courtyard. Many families who live in Pakistani cities share a courtyard with other families.

dialects (DY-uh-lekts)
Dialects are different forms of a language that are used in different regions of a country. Many dialects are spoken in Pakistan.

fast (FAST)
To fast means going without eating for a certain period of time. Muslims fast from sunrise to sunset each day during the month of Ramadan.

Hindus (HIN-dooz)
People who practice the Hindu religion are called Hindus. Many Hindus live in India, but few are found in Pakistan.

irrigated (EER-ih-gayt-ed)
When water is pumped onto dry farmland, the land is irrigated. Crops are able to grow in Pakistan because of irrigation.

Muslim (MUHS-lihm)
A person who follows the teachings of Islam is called a Muslim. Most Pakistanis are Muslims.

prophet (PROF-et)
A prophet is someone who tells a message that he or she believes has come from God. Muhammad was a prophet.

remains (ri-MAYNZ)
Remains are the parts of something that was once alive. Remains can also be bodies of people or animals that have died.

Index

To Find Out More

BOOKS

Black, Carolyn. *Pakistan the People.* New York: Crabtree, 2002.

Caldwell, John C. *Pakistan.* Broomall, Penn.: Chelsea House, 2000.

Hoyt-Goldsmith, Diane, and Lawrence Migdale (illustrator). *Celebrating Ramadan.* New York: Holiday House, 2001.

WEB SITES

Visit our home page for lots of links about Pakistan:
http://www.childsworld.com/links.html

Note to parents, teachers, and librarians: We routinely verify our Web links to make sure they're safe, active sites—so encourage your readers to check them out!